How to Have a Great Marriage

(Avoid Divorce and Keep Your Family)

By

Vincent A. Omoamilor

About the Author

Vincent Omoamilor is a trained counselor and a professional who over the past decade has had so much interest in helping people sustain and keep their marriages.

This book was created due to his passion for the family unit.

He is happily married with children.

Appreciation

I want to say thank you to the management and staff of Biblioteca Chimico-Biologica di Santa Maria delle Grazie, Biblioteca Comunale Ariostea, and Palazzo Del Vescovo-Biblioteca Comunale Giorgio Bassani – all in Ferrara Province, Italy – for providing the enabling environment for me to complete the writing of this book.

A special thank you to my wife for her support and encouragement all through the phase of writing this book, and to my wonderful kids. I love you all.

Also, thank you to my friends and family members. I really appreciate your contributions.

All glory be unto God Almighty.

Book Description

How To Have A Great Marriage is a book that covers in detail, matters relating to family and marriage and it gives you guidance on:

- How to choose a spouse,

- Solving marital issues,

- Avoiding divorce and saving your marriage from collapse, and

- Having a great family.

With the current high rate of divorce, driven by modern-day challenges in this technologically advanced generation, the institution of marriage is becoming less attractive to most people. This leaves them questioning its relevance.

This book is meant for the single people who are ready to marry, married couples who intend to spice up their marriage or couples who are facing marital challenges, and those whose marriages are on the verge of divorce. It will help you to navigate through those issues that may confront you or you are currently facing, ranging from making the decision to get married and dating to different stages of your marriage.

Read this book thoroughly and follow the guidelines and suggestions, as they will make you have a great family life.

Table Of Contents

INTRODUCTION

The divorce rate around the world has reached an astronomically high of all time and it as if what is considered as the traditional marriage (composing of two adults – man and woman) is under attack, as other forms of marriages (for example, same-sex marriages and marriage to animals) are being promoted.

Marriage was created by God. The concept of marriage is God's own idea. Whatever the religious beliefs you adhere to, if you consciously dig deep, you will find out more about what the Creator intended marriage to be.

In the book of Genesis, it states: "Therefore a man shall leave his father and mother and be joined to his wife, and they shall become one flesh." (**Genesis 2:24**)

Proverb 18:22 noted that: "He who finds a wife finds a good thing and obtains favor from the LORD."

In the **Quran [24:32]** Muhammad writes: "You shall encourage those of you who are single to get married. They may marry the righteous among your male and female servants if they are poor. GOD will enrich them from His grace. GOD is Bounteous, Knower."

If God Himself instituted marriage, you will agree with me that God cannot be wrong. Also, notice how God links marriage with prosperity. For the Christian: "He who finds a wife finds a good thing" plus "He obtains favor from the LORD." For Muslims: "they may marry the righteous among your male and female servants if they are poor. God will enrich them from His grace". That means that as humans, we are the ones that are certainly getting it wrong about marriage. As a result of this, the family unit in a society is gradually dying.

Family values are rapidly dwindling due to changing cultures and technology, as the growth of self-love fueled by social media influence is on the rise. The internet has redirected and created (which it is still doing) new means of communication: borderless interactions, simple and easy form and means of communication that are available 24/7. Instead of these available means of communication and technologies being used to strengthen the family, it has rather led to a diminishing bond within the family structure. For a world which has been reduced to a global village (with the advent of the internet) with much cultural influence from around the world, a more perceptional definition of what an ideal marriage, home and family should be is taking a different dimension.

An extract from Lumen in an article entitled Family, in defining and explaining the marriage context, noted that "marriage fulfills many other functions: it can establish the legal father of a woman's child; establish joint property for the benefit of children; or establish a relationship between the families of the husband and wife. These are only some examples; the family's function varies by society. The primary function of the family is to ensure the continuation of society, both biologically through procreation, and socially through socialization...."

The traditional family or the nuclear family comprises of a man, woman and their children. The man and woman are married and it's the marriage that creates an institution that protects and provides care for the children. The family has the most influence on a child's life. The importance and role of a nuclear family in the sustenance and growth of society are enormous. The high rate of divorce and parental failure can be linked to decaying societal morals and values. The more successful the family unit, the better the general society will be.

Therefore, we must make conscious efforts at ensuring divorce rates are reduced and the nuclear family is sustained while also encouraging married adults to be good parents.

This book will try to address some of these issues that are destroying marriages and families. It will first aim to examine the dating stage, for as it is, a lot of marriages could have been saved if proper caution and decisions were taken at this stage. Most failed marriages are due to challenges that can be traced to when the

Vincent A. Omoamilor

spouses were dating. After looking at the dating phase, we then gradually discuss marriage, touching various issues and areas that couples should monitor, be mindful of and take all necessary actions on. Then we will explore some of the major challenges in marriages and consider what can be the possible best solution to alleviate their effects.

Pope John XXIII - "The family is the first essential cell of human society."

(CHAPTER ONE)

THE DECISION TO MARRY

1 Corinthians 7:2 – "Nevertheless, because of sexual immorality, let each man have his own wife, and let each woman have her own husband."

The above quote means that the decision to get married is a good decision. However, what you need to know is if such a decision is right for you. Let us delve into this phase to help you analyze your decisions and choices.

Although this book is about marriage and the nuclear family – for the singles in the dating phase and/or pre-marriage phase – it will help you make better decisions. For those who are married, this stage may be where your possible current marital challenges may have originated from. You may want to take a retrospective view of your marital journey so far to see how to make amends or to resolve those challenges and forge a better future for your family.

Probably there is this wonderful person in your life or you just met him or her. Interaction between the two of you is getting intense and it looks like the relationship is heading towards marriage. Then you should examine your interactions with that person more seriously, possibly "interviewing" and getting to know them further. An organization that may want to employ you will take you through a series of tests and interviews. How much more you when you desire to take a life-long journey with someone. I know you may want to consider most of your time with this person for a fun period, but after all the fun, then come realities of life. You can be compatible in times of fun. In fact, there is rarely non-compatibility in fun. Almost everybody likes fun. But are you both compatible with life's realities? Can you cope with such a personality in the future?

But before meeting your spouse, have you given a proper thought to the idea of marriage? Do you really understand what marriage is all about? Does this marriage concept fit into your future goals and aspirations? Are you really a family kind of person? Do you really need to get married? Societal values, morals and religion encourage us to get married as adults. But the truth of it is, you are better off not getting married than for your marriage to end in divorce after a few days, weeks, months or years.

Traci Porterfield, an HR Consultant, states that "Dating in today's world can be complicated. With more and more dating sites and limited opportunities to meet someone on-the-go, the whole situation can feel a little overwhelming, even exhausting."

Your ability to self-examine yourself and answer some of the basic marital questions will set the ball rolling for you and give you an idea of your level of preparedness and the kind of spouse you will set out to look for.

You must understand that not everyone you will meet can fit into your kind of requirements for a spouse. So, you must also learn how to put a stop to whatever exists between you and the person that does not match your target once you discover that you are a mismatch. Allowing emotions, sentiments and lust to get the better of you, by staying or dragging forward a bad relationship, may not end well in the future.

You will be making a big mistake by ending up getting married out of pity or a feeling of indebtedness over a favor or some benefits you enjoyed from the person you were dating. If it is a favor, just find a way to reimburse the individual. If you must or just feel forever grateful to the person that rendered such favor to you, repay them, rather than use your entire life to pay for it. That is what you will be doing if you marry out of pity, guilt or a feeling of indebtedness; living the remaining parts of your life as a payment for the favor that was rendered to you, especially when the person who rendered such assistant did not sacrifice their lives to help you.

Let us consider those typical questions one after the other, not necessarily answering them the perfect way, but trying to do some level of justice to them as much as we can and as time can permit.

WHAT IS MARRIAGE?

Marriage is the union of two adults for the purpose of building a family. As we stated earlier, it was instituted by God.

"Marriage fulfills many other functions: It can establish the legal father of a woman's child; establish joint property for the benefit of children; or establish a relationship between the families of the husband and wife. These are only some examples; the family's function varies by society." – **Lumen's** Family. We quoted this earlier at the introductory stage.

Encyclopedia Britannica – "Marriage, a legally and socially sanctioned union, usually between a man and a woman, that is regulated by laws, rules, customs, beliefs, and attitudes that prescribe the rights and duties of the partners and accords status to their offspring (if any)."

It is these societal customs, beliefs and attitudes that are now affecting most marriages, as there have been changing values and norms coupled with the effect of technology.

Catholic Education – "As many people acknowledge, marriage involves: first, a comprehensive union of spouses; second, a special link to children; and third, norms of permanence, monogamy, and exclusivity. All three elements point to the conjugal understanding of marriage."

From these various definitions and explanations above, the key components of marriage are:

1.   Intimacy between two consenting adults (man and woman) to form a single entity

2.   A permanent union (forever till death) and

3.   A protective institution for their children

Before getting into marriage, you need to ask yourself if you are willing and ready to establish a relationship that covers these three components stated above. If your answer is a no to just one of them, then you actually do not need to get married or it is not yet time for you and you need to do some additional homework on yourself to be ready in the future.

Let us look a little bit at some of the wrong reasons people engage in marriages or some of the wrong foundations of marriages.

WRONG FOUNDATIONS OF MARRIAGES

There are several wrong reasons (or not the ideal reasons) why people get married.

• Societal (parental and peer) Pressures

Do not let society, your parents, friends and family members pressure you into marriage. If this is a union that you are not ready for, please try to not enter it until you are ready. Because, in the long run, you are the only one who is going to be living a frustrated and unhappy life, not them. In some countries, societal norms have created a parameter. Once you have attained XYZ status in life, the next step people encourage you to take is to get married. If you are yet to do that, there may be myriads of questions and advice from all angles, encouraging and pushing you to get married even when you know that you are not ready. It is not that this is a bad idea, it's just that in as much as the society is expecting this from you, you also need to be prepared for it. Do not jump into marriage unprepared (emotionally, spiritually, financially and psychologically). It is better to try your best and wade off these pressures than to let them push you into what you are not ready for. Apart from the financial consequences of a divorce, there is also an emotional effect it has on separated couples. Matters get more complicated when kids are involved. That is why you need to try your best to avoid these damages.

•   Material Things/Social Status

When you read further into this book, you will discover that when couples are able to pull their finances together and manage it properly, it places them in better financial standing than they would have been independent. On a very rare occasion do people who get married have this objective in mind. Most often, if the intention of the marriage was for financial gain, it is

                                          Vincent A. Omoamilor

considered a parasitic relationship, where one member wants to use the other person's financial status for their own gain. In no time, such marriages may crumble mainly due to other marital challenges. This is not to say other marriages that are well-intentioned do not face crisis and failure; in fact, no marriage is conflict-free. But it is important you place your marriage on the right foundation. If financial success is so paramount to you, let me tell you that you can be financially successful on your own without getting married. This is possible if you are dedicated, focused and committed to becoming financially buoyant, either in your choice of career or through other ventures.

- Sex

Sex is important in a marriage. But basing your marriage solely on sex will be the wrong foundation for you to lay. Sex with a partner will not always be exciting as it was normally at the initial stage. At some point, it will get boring in the marriage, especially when deliberate efforts are not being made to continue to spice up the sexual life of the couple and when sex is your only interest. That is why marriages that are solely built on sex fails. I always ask: after the great sex, what next? Yes, sex serves various purposes such as sex in a marriage for procreation, sex as an "icing" on marriage with great intimacy, sex for fun or sex for building a marital bond. As mentioned earlier, sex is important in a marriage – there's no doubt about that! Later we will dwell on its importance. But marriage is more than just sex. Do not try to hook someone into a marriage with sex. They may lust initially, but at some point in that marriage, all the lust will be cleared, and that person will most likely hate you with passion when he or she found out they have been deceived or lured into marriage they do not want. This is not good for a marriage.

- Having Children

Going by the definitions and explanations of marriage above, children are a part of a family. But there are those who believe the usefulness of a man or a woman is purely for making babies and they will solely go into marriage just to have children. In this modern era where "Baby Mama/Father" is common and acceptable, people just want to have one or two kids and quit the marriage. This situation is not nice when the other spouse is not aware of their intentions. Such an act is horrible. Once they achieve their aims, they look for some form of excuses to end the marriage, making the other spouse feel like a failure or have some heavy form of self-guilt. It is bad to get someone tied up with you while having such an agenda in your heart without them knowing. If all you wanted was a child, then there is no need to get another person's future hooked up with your agenda. In fact, technology has made it possible for a single adult to have children on their own. To help matters, you can tell your spouse what your intentions are when you meet them or during courtship and let him/her agree or grant consent. Some may even agree to do this with you without getting married, and you will have your child and both adults will be happy than leaving the other person emotionally wrecked or with a heartbreak. The responsibilities of raising a child/children can be very daunting, and where there is a lack of intimacy and shared responsibilities in the home, there could be frustration and depression among spouses.

A balance and good marriage can get you social status, wealth, fantastic sex life and great kids, all wrapped up in a bundle. Basing your marital decision solely on one or two of these reasons is where the challenge stems from; because other marital issues may and will overwhelm them during the duration of the marriage. Take time to look at these issues concisely and holistically and ensure you are ready for marriage and you do not base your marriage solely on any of the above-listed rationale or any other reasons that are not morally correct. Then you also need to access your preparedness for the institution of marriage. Get yourself emotionally, spiritually, psychologically and financially prepared for marriage.

After you have carried out your research by asking yourself all these and many other questions, and you conclude or realize that you are ready for marriage, your next line of action is to get a compatible partner and one that you love. Marrying someone you love (and who also returns the affection) is not enough to sustain your marriage. In fact, some argue that initial love before marriage only lasts for about two years or thereabout. The love that exists in a marriage, in the long run, is what was consciously built overtime during the marriage by both spouses. If both spouses are not consciously building love and intimacy, then the marriage will dissipate in the long run.

Compatibility does not mean you both must think alike. Being able to understand, support, encourage and get along well with each other, is the crux of it all; as long as you or your spouse is not doing anything illegal, immoral or humanly degrading. It will be frustrating and discouraging later in life when the major/main source from which you are to receive support and encouragement becomes your greatest antagonist or obstacle. When it comes to certain projects and agendas in life, there is nothing more important than a supporting spouse because, throughout life, you are going to need such support. It is like the strength of an enemy or friend within, so things could really be that frustrating and discouraging or exciting and motivating.

In the next chapter, we will delve a little bit into some steps you need to take to guide you towards making a better decision related to choosing a spouse.

Elizabeth Gilbert, in Committed: A Skeptic Makes Peace with Marriage stated that "People always fall in love with the most perfect aspects of each other's personalities. Who wouldn't? Anybody can love the most wonderful parts of another person. But that's not the clever trick. The really clever trick is this: can you accept the flaws? Can you look at your partner's faults honestly and say, 'I can work around that. I can make something out of it?' Because the good stuff is always going to be there, and it's always going to be pretty and sparkly, but the crap underneath can ruin you."

(CHAPTER TWO)

MEETING YOUR SPOUSE [DATING]

You now have this special person in your life that you are dating and the relationship seems to be getting stronger, then it is time to be mindful and intentional about your dating activities. When you go for a date, when you visit each other, whenever you are both together, use it as an opportunity to ask questions, study and understand the person you are planning to spend the rest of your life with. This is very important. As mentioned in the previous chapter, use your time with your husband/wife to be, as an interview/investigation/observation session. Try to always live in the present and trust your instinct during this phase, especially if it has been true to you in the past. Nobody is saying that you should not have fun, but do not be too carried away as not to be conscious of the immediate environment when you both are together. In between chats, ask as many purposeful and intentional questions as you can. Try to ensure your questions are relevant to the goal or agenda in mind which is marriage and those questions are precise. Take note of the response or answers you get when you ask those vital and crucial questions relating to their marital agenda. Because you are going to be cross-examining those answers in the future with realities, ensure that you have not been fed with pre-meditated or tailor-made responses.

Outlined below are some of the areas to base questions on.

1)   **Family and background**. Growing up experiences, family history and background can reveal a lot about someone's beliefs, morals and values because these factors will have a lot of impact on your home in the future, in the event that you both are married. There will come a time in your marriage that a decision about an event or something, will simply boil down to the morals and beliefs of you both. This can be a major source of conflict in a marriage. Raise questions that border on morals and beliefs. Ask questions about their parents, whether both parents are still alive and married and what is or was their relationship like

(yes, let them talk about it). These might give you an idea of the factors that contributed to how they perceive marriage and family.

a.   **Siblings**. How many are they? What position is he/she in their family (for example, first or last or middle child)? Is he or she from a polygamous or monogamous family? How was and is the relationship between them and their siblings? What are their names and their meanings, especially if they are native names in a dialect that is not of your own?

In some cultures, the position of your spouse in his or her family matters. Firstborn versus lastborn can be a challenge and lastborn versus lastborn may work better in different cultural settings. For instance, when a firstborn who has responsibilities to attend to the needs of his or her siblings get married to another firstborn with similar responsibilities, that could result in a lot of demands on the family in the future.

b.   **Growing up experiences**. What has he/she gone through in life – as a child, adolescent and even as an adult? What about their neighborhoods, categories of friends and experiences, type of schools attended and some of their school experiences?

The life experience of someone who grew up in the ghetto will certainly be different from the one raised in an urban city center. This can affect one's behavior later on in life.

c.   **Adult life**. Work-life (please find out what he/she does for a living, but do not be carried away. You can even pay a visit to his or her place of work during working hours) and know his or her type of colleagues. What does your spouse think about raising children? This won't be relevant if you are not planning on having kids. Discuss typical societal issues with your fiancée, general issues around the world. See whether they have any understanding of these issues and what their thought pattern is like.

You are better off when you end up with someone with a broad view about life who can see things from different perspectives, not a one-track minded individual.

I know this may sound like you are carrying out a whole lot of investigations, but hey, because this is the person you intend to spend the rest of your life with, then it is worth it.

If you pay vivid attention to these responses, chances are, some of the challenges you both may face later in the marriage, may likely be avoided with the understanding of each other growing up, family background, experiences and thought patterns or mindset.

2) **Finance**. When it comes to marriage, finance is a very important factor. Lots of divorce cases can be traced to financial issues. There are studies that state that about 21% of divorce cases are related to financial issues. Spend time

asking questions about their financial habits. How do they see money, in terms of beliefs and value for money? What are their spending habits, savings culture, loan history and debt profile (please check it)? Do they have the notion of clean or dirty money? Are they concerned with the source of money or he/she believes money is money, irrespective of where the money is gotten from? This may not be a nice mindset about money, so one should be concerned about the source of money – whether illegal, amoral or through crime?

Having a good idea of your spouse's perceptions about money is very important. You may also start a conversation about how you both will plan your future finances. Not necessarily embarking on that now, because it may sound too early, but just a tip of such conversation can make you have a filler of what the future may look like.

3)   **Difficult seasons in life**. Even those that are having life on a roller coaster, also have what they classify as their difficult seasons. Life cannot be "beds of roses" all the way. There comes a period or periods when things will/may be rough in your marriage. While you are on the background questions, try to find out how they handled difficult seasons in their life. Questions such as "Have you ever had difficult times in your life?" can lead to a lot of discussions for that day. If the person says he or she has not experienced such times in life, paint a scenario for

them and ask what they did or would rather do when in such circumstances.

4)   **Trust/lies**. Is the word "trust" important to him or her? To have a good home, there must be trust. Lies should be out of the context because the moment lies comes into a home, trust flies away. Taking time to discuss these topics can give a guide of what to expect in the future. Be on the guard, by trying to confirm intermittently if his/her actions match their words. There is no gain repeating the general saying, "Action speaks louder than words."

5)   **Sex**. Talk about sex in your series of discussions. The fact that you are discussing sex does not necessarily mean you both are about to indulge in the act.

                              Vincent A. Omoamilor

Have a guided discussion on this topic because of its sensitivity, especially when you do not plan to be intimate with each other soon. Conversations around this area of human life can be misinterpreted. Some may assume that because you raised a topic about sex, you want to have sex with them, and such conversations can throw up a lot of issues. So, tread cautiously when you are in this area. Try to find out: (i) how he/she sees sex (ii) what is his/her beliefs about it (iii) his/her level of sexual desires and activeness (iv) sex with animals...what is his/her opinion on this topic (v) Sex toys...how does she/he sees it (vi) gay and lesbian issues...what does he/she think about it? It may also do you some good to have conversations that are centered around oral sex. These conversations are important because you may not be able to change your spouse's views later on in the marriage.

6) **Conflicts and disputes resolutions in their life**. Observing how people resolve conflicts and how they react in times of crisis, tells a lot about their personality. Are they humble enough to acknowledge their wrong? When they are wrong, do they apologize? Or do they hold on to their ego? There are people who just react to the spur of the moment; this is not ideal. The presence of humility is a good sign. Check their emotions and empathy towards issues. These can cause challenges later on in the marriage.

7)   **Selflessness,   faithfulness, commitments and loyalty**. Like we just mentioned, humility is key. Is your spouse humble and submissive? A woman needs a man who is faithful to her and loves her unconditionally. While a man needs a woman that is committed and loyal to him. Cheap words/phrases – such as "we are human," "it is blood that runs in the vein," – are used to defend certain acts that stem from undisciplined personality. Is your man faithful? It should be an important question to answer as a lady. Or, as a man, will your woman go all the way for and with you?

8)   **Level of Fitness (physically and mentally)**. This mainly depends on what you are attracted to. But a physically and

mentally fit person can give you an advantage over a lot of things in your marriage. The ability to withstand marital pressures and demand and not be calling for a divorce at the slightest provocation boils down to the strengths of your spouse's mentality. The level of your spouse's intelligence can also contribute a great deal to the amount of wealth your family possesses and control.

9) **Lastly, biological compatibility**. It is important to check your level of biological compatibility before hooking up with this person. Check your blood group, genotype and fertility level. You want to avoid giving birth to a "sickler" or struggling to give birth (in cases where a spouse may have challenges with his/her

reproductive organs) when you have the intention of doing so in your marriage, as the inability to bear children can also lead to divorce. There are factors that could be beyond your control. But for those you can do something about, please do it.

In all your assessments, find out how much of themselves they understand and how much of yourself you understand. This is very important. How well does the person in question understand him/herself for them to be able to accommodate others? Someone who is still finding it hard to understand themselves may find it difficult relating well with their other half.

When you have responses and answers to these questions and others not highlighted here, you have an idea of where your spouse stands in these areas. You now have to take your time matching his/her actions with their words. That is how to confirm that they were not blabbing when they were responding to you. There are things they will say or do consciously or subconsciously, take note of them... those are your real pointers and indicators, do not ignore them or shrug them aside.

Luke 6:45 states that "a good man out of the good treasure of his heart brings forth good and an evil man out of the evil treasure of his heart brings forth evil. For out of the abundance of the heart, his mouth speaks (and acts)."

If you take your time observing your spouse, there are signs that will be displayed that you should not ignore, specifically, the warning or danger signs. Listen to them when they are happy or extremely sad. People tend to pour out the real contents of their hearts in times of extreme emotions.

Try to manage your emotions at the early stage of a relationship. It is the emotions that often get in the way of logical reasoning and that is what prevents a lot of people from taking the right actions after noticing the danger signs.

Controlling the rate of sex at the early stage of dating is important. If you can abstain from sex entirely during this period until you are sure and have decided about your future together then, better for you. This helps you to see the true personality of the person you are dealing with. On the issue of sex, which is a bigger topic, if you are female, your loss is always higher. From unwanted pregnancy (because you are the one that will get pregnant when there is a mistake) to abortion (you are the one that will need endure the abortion if pregnancy occurs) to your physical and emotional loss (your physical composition will certainly not remain the same after undergoing certain stage/s of sexual activities, especially when pregnancies and abortions were involved) and other health and even spiritual implications), you are the one who stands to lose more than the male.

When it comes to negotiation, the sets and value of instruments at your disposal,

 Vincent A. Omoamilor

determine what you get at the negotiation table. The same goes for relationships that lead to marriage. If you're female, sex is or could be your strongest tool to negotiate terms for a better marriage commitment in a relationship. When you play this card at the start of an affair, it loses its value. Try to ensure you get a better commitment to the relationship before playing the sex card.

Watch your greed: what am I getting from this relationship? These are the factors that can blind your mind and hinder your logical and best decisions thoughts. So, you ignore what is so glaring in the relationship because of the gifts and material things you are enjoying.

Then pressure: you can see the signs, you felt something is not right in this relationship, you know some of these things you cannot cope with them in the long run, but the pressure is on you. Note that it is better you did not enter into that marriage at all and avoid future heartbreaks than you ignore all the danger signs and go into the marriage. Then after a short while, you are out and back to square one.

With the majority of the challenges you may face later in your marriage, most often the signs were always there at the dating phase of the relationship. If you can pay attention enough and take the right actions immediately as you notice them, you may be able to avoid early divorce if not able to avoid it entirely.

Do your homework when you meet your spouse and take the right actions immediately if you notice a red flag.

After you have done all your studies and assessment of your spouse, before you conclude whether to marry them or not, perform two simple tasks:

i.   Note that you are marrying his/her personality. So, strip all other added advantages you have noticed on the person, like financial strength, beauty/good looks and the likes (although all these factors put together makes up who they are). But if those things are taken away from them, are you fine with their personality (character and behavior) and can you live with them forever?

ii.   All the problems/challenges you have perceived or noticed, even the little ones, magnify them all and add these challenges to this person, can you live with them forever?

If the answers to these two tasks are YES, you have greatly reduced the probability of marital failure.

Remember, subtract the benefits and add the magnified perceived and known problems.

Before the marriage, discuss with each other extensively. Ensure that there are no damaging secrets between you both. Do not give chances to future blackmails.

Later, when your marriage may be looking sweet, those are the times when hidden dirty secrets tend to resurface. The damages they may cause to your family will be much. If at all this kind of problem resurface in the future, do not make the mistake of taking dirty actions or telling bigger lies in order to cover and keep old secrets. It will boomerang in the long run and create bigger havoc. Treat the issue immediately.

Benjamin Sledge – "Marriage is a covenant, not a legal contract that lays out terms, but a mutual understanding that regardless of performance, you are still all in. It is a love that understands that the essence of marriage is a sacrificial commitment to the good of the other. It's unit not just duty and passion, but emotions and promises."

[CHAPTER 3]

THE MARRIAGE AND

IMMEDIATELY AFTER

Now, that you have made your decision to tie the knot, there could be a lot of pressure. The biggest and most frequent source of pressure comes from family members. With family (and sometimes friends) pressure can ruin your wedding or marriage ceremonies as it has done to others.

Whatever the choices are, ensure that both of you are on the same page. Do not let a ceremony of one day erase your expected future joy with your spouse. One area where problems normally stem from is trying to create what some tag "the talk of the town event." Do not try to do this with your marriage if you do not have the ability to do so. The life ahead of you is more important. You may want to make it as memorable as possible to the best of your ability, but if the elegance is going to create quarrel between you and your spouse which may threaten the peace of your planned home, then there is no need for it; nothing is worth it. Making your marriage memorable is not a bad idea but putting your marriage in a danger zone to achieve this is not worth it. Start by coming up with a budget. On average, what you would like to spend all together in the wedding ceremony. Even the high and mightiest of society make budgets and work within that budget. So, yours will not be an exception.

This is the season/time when family members of both spouses get to interact with each other for probably the first time. There are bound to be disagreements between the two families, but these disagreements should be managed properly.

Spouses are usually under pressure and their bad emotional side tends to show. Can you still accommodate calling off the marriage at this phase if you noticed any danger signs? Then be on the lookout. Do not ignore these signs when you see them, pay attention; at some point or the other in your marriage, family pressures will surface, and these ugly sides of your spouse may likely come out again.

The general phrase is that the marriage ceremony is a once in a lifetime event, so it must be big and in a grand style. True, it is a once in a lifetime event, but you do not have to impress anybody with your marriage ceremonies if it may cost you and your spouse your happiness and jeopardize your union now or in the future. So, there is no need for an event that is beyond your capacity. Stay within your financial strength. It is advisable not to take a loan for such a celebration, no matter how tempting the urge may be. At the early stage of marriage, it is better for your family to have as much financial assets as possible, either saved or invested, to support the family especially when you start having kids. When couples start having kids, financial demands begin to increase, mostly when the kids are set for schooling (for countries where early childhood education is not free and expensive) there tends to be a lot of financial burdens on the family.

Understanding that the marriage preparation phase is one of the sources of marriage pressure and taking proper steps and actions to mitigate any havoc the pressure from this phase may cause is very crucial.

Some of the challenges you may need to take care of at this phase of the relationship to ensure you do not jeopardize your lifetime of marriage are:

I.   Properly Managing the Expectations and Relationships of Both Spouses' Family Members

You are both adults and about to begin a new chapter of your life. This is one of the roles in which you may start demonstrating your level of maturity. It is heartbreaking when you see some spouse crying, yelling at each other, and some even go as far as threatening to cancel the wedding on the day due to these pressures. What can help you both is to have a discussion with your parents, letting them understand that this is your event. How both families relate with each other as well at this stage is also an important aspect that should not be ignored. You understand your family members better than your spouse. Your spouse should also have a good knowledge of his or her family. Managing how the two families interact with each other can be managed from the understanding point of both spouses.

II.   The Financial Demand and Budget

If proper planning and budgeting are not done, and carefully keeping within such budget, or a little stretch from the planned budget, there may be future financial challenges that may put holes in the marriage in the long run. Event Planners, friends or family members may try to make you overshoot your planned budget beyond your limit; do not fall for it. You have a whole lifetime to live after the marriage ceremony and wedding day.

Financial demand and pressure are one of the major factors that crash most marriages. Hanging one on your neck at this early stage of your marriage is a danger you should avoid at the beginning.

III. Marriage Preparation Pressures as it Unmask Negative Signals

There are lots of pressures while spouses prepare for their wedding ceremonies. These pressures tend to reveal some of the concealed negative signals on both spouses. Communicate with each other and see how possible those evolving issues are attended to and are being resolved. It is important that you both have a workable conflict resolution pattern. If you don't, create one, so that in the future, when such or other conflicts arise, you both will resolve to the resolution pattern you have created.

While you are preparing for marriage, a lot of things can evolve. You may see a personality that is entirely different from the person you have been dating. Maybe due to the pressures at that moment or some thought of we are getting married, they feel a less need to be pretentious or hide certain secrets; unmasking their true personality. If you find yourself in this kind of circumstance, count yourself lucky. Remember: the knot is not yet tied. If you discover issues that you may not be able to cope with for a lifetime, act by pulling the plug. A broken relationship is better than a broken marriage. Be sure not to overreact as well on your part. If it is a minor issue that can be managed, then put efforts at resolving it immediately. Those little negatives you saw and noticed, may likely be aggravated in the future. Adults rarely change formed habits when it is needed. They will certainly change in the future when you both are married, but such changes happen gradually over time due to events and circumstances. Even if you cannot resolve all the challenges, let them be issues you can live with in the long run in case you are unable to change your spouse. Carrying a problem into a marriage by wishing away the challenge is not the best.

IMMEDIATELY AFTER THE MARRIAGE

Welcome to another phase of life: the era of realities. We will now focus on marriage and the family unit from this point onward.

Immediately after the wedding, then comes marriage. Unwrapping the gift items, counting the financial gift from the event and deciding what exactly to do with them may cause some quarrels to develop. Please do not let quarrel ensue between you and your husband/wife from this task, as this is almost like a husband and wife's first decision-making activity. All the decisions you both have been making together before now were being taken as adults who were dating. But now it is different even if you do not see it that way. Your spouse may be holding the mindset at this point (rights and privileges have changed). You both should decide together what to do with each gift item. A unanimous decision is better as this builds trust and confidence at the start.

Financial Gift

Who takes, keeps or does what, should be agreed upon by both spouses. When husband and wife agreed on a line of action, it tends to avoid misunderstandings. Even when you are not sure or confident about what you both agreed to spend the money on, give your partner the benefit of doubt. Do not always insist things must be done according to your preference or even go as far as calling family members over this small issue.

Honeymoon

The general practice is that after the marriage ceremony, the couple will head for a honeymoon. It is not a rule or a process in marriage. It is just a practice that is now generally considered to be a big ideal or overexaggerated. Honeymoon gives couples an opportunity for them to explore each other and know themselves more, thereby building intimacy. It is not compulsory, although highly recommended. It does not necessarily have to be exotic, in a long-distance or a foreign country. If you do not have the financial muscles for this, do not wear yourself out. You are already into the marriage which is a lifelong journey. You will have more opportunities in the future to embark on such trips, so you can postpone it or have a simple plan that will enable you and your spouse to spend time together (stay out of the world…away from distractions). Just live your life according to what works for you.

But if you happen to go for one, use it as a period of planning your family, building intimacy and understanding each other better. Not just for fun. Don't get on that cruise and just cruise through the time. All the questions you have asked during dating, with the answers you have been given, keep matching those answers with actions and continue to know your spouse better. It might be too early to be noticing changes but concentrating on that moment is better than getting carried away.

Make plans about your home. Plan about:

o   <u>Finance</u>

Depending on the financial position and status of each spouse, whether both spouses are working (earning), you should make plans on how your home will be funded on the basis of recurrent and capital expenditures...who will bring A, B or C and who will be financially responsible for certain things in the house, like major expenditure and household items and upkeep? How will the money be spent? How will you attend to extended family member needs, request, etc.?

o   <u>Babies</u>

Make plans for them. Are you having kids? How many do you both plan to have? When? In terms of spacing, what is your gap between each child? When the kids start arriving, will a spouse quit his or her job to take care of the children and the home? Are there financial plans in the event of this happening? Making those plans at the early stage of marriage is good, so that in the future when these issues are evident, all you will be doing is referring to your blueprint.

o   <u>Who to live in your home</u>

The third person in your home can sometimes be the external eye in your house monitoring activities. So, you must

                                    Vincent A. Omoamilor

be careful about who you accommodate in your home. Be it extended family member or a house help, be careful of the person you let into your home and this should not be taken for granted.

o <u>Career</u>

Plan how you both will be able to fit your schooling, career or business into your marital life. You may not be able to follow these plans in a strict sense but having a guide will do a lot of good in the future.

o <u>Nothing can be replaced with intimacy in your home</u>

Connect with each other and build stronger bonds. You will need this in the future. Work out your dispute resolution pattern. No matter how sweet your home is, there is always bound to be misunderstanding between you and your spouse. One golden rule you can use in your home is, "no matter the level of argument, misunderstanding or quarrel, do not break communication with each other."

Like we said earlier in this section, it is not a must you and your spouse will embark on honeymoon immediately after marriage, especially if your finances cannot accommodate the kind of arrangements you prefer. But if you both had to go, use it to organize and plan the future of your home. Leave your work at the office and avoid other things that may distract both of you including your phones and mobile devices. Try to learn about each other and know yourself more. Use this time to bond properly and build your level of intimacy.

Jane Austen, Sense and Sensibility: "It is not time or opportunity that is to determine intimacy; —it is disposition alone. Seven years would be insufficient to make some people acquainted with each other, and seven days are more than enough for others."

[CHAPTER FOUR]

COMMUNICATION IN MARRIAGE

Cherie Carter Scott – "Without good communication, a relationship is merely a hollow vessel carrying you along on a frustrating journey fraught with the perils of confusion, projection, and misunderstanding."

Communication is an act of imparting or exchanging information by speaking, writing or a means of sending or receiving information.

Communication is very important in a marriage. This is a major factor that will make the two individuals function well together. In a marriage, you have two adults, who may have been raised differently, coming together as one. They think differently, respond to things differently and perceive/understand things differently. Communication is vital for couples to act and live as one entity. Most often, minor marital challenges will escalate as a result of communication break down between spouses. Developing and maintaining good and healthy communication can help couples avoid a lot of challenges in their marriage.

For starters, clear the "F-words" from your communication language. This is important because very soon, the kids will start coming and children are very fast at picking up words from their parents. As a couple, you also need to choose your preferred language of communication at home, especially if you are both bi-lingual.

Stephan Labossiere – "Let communication be the seed that you water with honesty and love. So that it may produce a happy, fulfilling, and successful relationship."

Some key attributes or habits that can help you in strengthening your communication with your spouse are:

• **Asking questions and listening**. Dr. S. Greg, the author of Crazy Little Thing Called Marriage, said, "Take joy in rediscovering your spouse over and over."

Ask your spouse questions to know him or her. Ask questions about things you do not know and understand. When they are talking to you or responding to your questions or even asking you for anything, listen. Communication is more than spoken words. Pay attention to both the unspoken communication and reactions. Develop passionate and emphatic listening habits. You must manage your sense of ridicule when your spouse is talking to you so that this does not affect his or her confidence. Getting the message your husband/wife is trying to pass across is also vital. In addition, try to sense your spouse's emotions, either body language, facial expression or spoken words and sense words he or she could not say. Eye contact during important conversations is also good.

Avoid yelling at each other. When the argument is getting heated, one good step you can take is to pause and take a little break away from that conversation. By the time you return, flaring emotions and nerves would have calmed a bit. Remember you cannot take back spoken words that hurt, which you might have said while you were angry.

• **Respect and appreciation**. There should be mutual respect in your marriage, and that is why it is important not to yell at your partner when you are talking to him or her. Always try to be calm in your conversation and communication, no matter how angry and infuriated you are towards your spouse. Let the words carry the message and keep the tone down.

Always remember not to use "F-words" or derogatory language toward your spouse no matter how angry you are.

On a regular basis, appreciate your spouse. Just tell him/her "Thank you" or "Well done." Tell them how grateful you are for what he/she has been doing and that you value them. One big mistake couples make is assuming or believing that they are already into the relationship and that there is no need to be making efforts in strengthening the love in their home. When you feel good, especially about an act or action by your spouse, tell her/him: "'Honey, thank you. I really do appreciate you," "My wife/husband, you are one in a million," or "Babe, I love you."

Say those things to your spouse and say them like you mean it, which you should. Express your love both in words and actions to your spouse. There can be no limit to which you can say the phrase "I love you." Except you do not have to be over exaggerative. Say it like you mean it and mean it as you say it.

•   **Corrections and criticism**. The general saying: "Open rebuke is better than secret love" does not apply in a marriage. Secret rebuke is the ideal way when it comes to marriage. When a spouse does or says something that you felt he or she should be corrected, if it is not some joke or casual statements, be mindful of where and how you do the correction. The best time and place to correct your spouse is when both of you are together alone; not in an abusive way or manner. If you feel you may likely forget while waiting for the right time, take a sheet of paper and write somewhere that you are likely to come across again.

- **Complaining and shaming.** Doing this to your spouse into trying to change them is wrong and most often, backfires. It may make the other person gets into a defensive and attack mode, instead of trying to understand what you are saying and making the right adjustment. Try to make them understand how important what you are saying is and that it is not a joke, instead of shouting and being abusive. Some experts suggest that you write down criticism and hand it over to your spouse.

Another approach is assuming the blame for the problem or make the correction suggestive. Starting with statements like, "Angel, I would have preferred if this is XYZ," "If I had known..." "I should have told you earlier," "It is my fault....." These kinds of phrases will most likely make them feel sympathetic rather than becoming defensive. For instance, your spouse cooked rice, and there was not enough salt. After tasting a spoon of the meal, you say, "Dear, it looks like this food needs more salt or what do you think?" When they understand what you said, a feeling of remorse might first engulf them, then they may smile and say, "Sorry, next time, I will ensure there is enough salt." Compared to when you say, in an angry and loud voice, "You do not know how to do anything. Not even to cook rice. You cannot cook it properly. This is tasteless." They will most likely think of how to insult you in return instead of trying to figure out why you are complaining.

•   **Trust and lies**. Being truthful and open to each other can help you build trust in your home. Trust is a very important ingredient in a home. A home looks more like a business venture when there is no trust. Each partner is trying to guide and protect their individual interest instead of the collective interest of both spouses. Half-truths are not truths when it comes to marriage. Your spouse deserves to know or hear the complete story, event or issue. Express your feelings to your spouse instead of hiding it. Tell him or her what you think or how you feel.

LIES

When it comes to communicating with your spouse, lying is not an option; not in any circumstance. When your spouse discovered you lied or have been lying to them, it becomes difficult for them to trust or believe you even when you are telling the truth. There is nothing like small lies; all lies are lies. Most often, circumstances or situations lead you to where you have to tell more lies to cover the initial lie you considered to be a small lie. A marriage without trust will suffer from intimacy. Couples begin to get suspicious of each other's actions and respond in disbelief. A series of lies leads to cheating, blackmail, extramarital affairs and before you know it, your marriage is on the brink of collapse – just because of a situation that would have been entirely avoided or nipped in the bud by just telling the truth from the start. Sometimes, the things we fear the most are non-existing. Our minds bring those things into existence. But this does not say you should ignore your instincts when there are clear and visible signs. Lingering suspicions of your spouse may lead to nagging and quarreling, which will starve the marriage of closeness as well as intimacy; then the marriage tears apart. Truthfulness and openness make couples easily believe each other and that is how trust is built in the home. The moment lies, deceits and secrecy are introduced in a relationship, trust flies out of the window. The other party begins to question every move, step and action, even the innocent ones.

If you desire to build better, stronger and long-lasting relationships, avoid trust breakers. They are the number one destroyers of marital relationships. It is okay to be vulnerable to your spouse; it is okay to be susceptible to him or her. As husband and wife, you do not have to be one solid unmovable rock when it comes to your spouse. Your vulnerability does not mean that you are weak. Risk it all until your spouse proves to you that he or she does not deserve that spot or position in your life.

                                     Vincent A. Omoamilor

SECRECY AND A WEAK LINK

Secrecy makes couples susceptible to temptation. Never allow yourself to be the weak link in your marriage and home. Have you ever had a chance to meet a couple in a situation where someone (either friend or relative) tries to create divisiveness or secrecy in order to use one of the spouses or take advantage of the family, and the couples make that person looks as bad as he/she or the schemer actually is? This can only happen when a spouse does not hide the issue from the other person or betray them. It is important to let your spouse know everything from the beginning; that is the ideal way of handling such matters. Allowing yourself to be the weak link into your home that led to the breakup of your marriage, may cause you more future regrets apart from the pain of having a broken home. Be careful about the amount of information you release about your family to a third party, whoever they are, except you are dealing with a professional who specializes in the matter and you are seeking help. You can easily forgive and forget certain wrong done to you by your husband/wife, and whatever the issue is will be resolved amicably between the two of you. But once some issues get to your family and friends, it will be hard for them to forget it or forgiving your spouse. They will elaborate on it and even add what has not even existed in the first place. When the issue between you and your spouse does not involve violence, infidelity or a life-threatening matter, it is better you try to resolve it between the two of you.

RELATING WITH OPPOSITE SEX

Managing relationships with the opposite sex who are friends or in-laws as long as the person is not a blood relative (assuming incest is out of the picture) are important. Because if care is not taken, you both can begin to develop feelings for each other and from that point, matters escalate. When you are at a point when you are no longer comfortable letting your spouse know about the conversation or activities with an opposite sex (who is friend or your wife/husband family member) or you are beginning to keep secrets of your activities with such person from your spouse, then it may be time for you to put a halt on that relationship. When you find yourself at a compromising point in a relationship with the opposite sex (or in fact with same-sex) that may jeopardize your marriage, cut it and move closer to your spouse; or at best, reveal all that has transpired between you and that person to your spouse (while also minding your spouse reactions). If what you get from this person is advice/counseling or some favor, especially from the opposite sex, just take the advice and leave or desist from receiving that favor or benefit from him/her.

GIFTS/KINDNESS AS A LOOPHOLE

Another angle of penetrating your home is through a disguised act of kindness (like we mentioned earlier). Always be careful with gifts and acts of kindness irrespective of the source. Ensure you tell your spouse to be on the safer side especially with gifts from the opposite sex. When he or she is sensing negative signals, do not ignore their warning or simply classify them as being jealous. Even if there are spouse that could be extremely jealous, their objections are worth considering, primarily because of the position they occupy. Also, go a step further to let the giver know that your spouse is or will be told of their gesture. Those with sinister intentions, always get uncomfortable with that idea. If you want to predict their intention, pay attention to how they react when you tell them that your spouse will be informed. Some will react by withdrawing from you, while some will jokingly or in a soft way try to tell or persuade you to keep it a secret. Some will scold you like you are a child. If you value your family and want to place your marriage and home on a safer side, ignore them and do the right thing. Do not accept the offer of secrecy between you and them. The person you should be sharing or keeping secrets with is your spouse. When such gifts and kindness are beginning to get too much, then it is time for you to withdraw and say NO to some of these gestures. The phrase "Conflict of Interest" is real. You will be surprised by how some little form of gift or kindness that may look as innocent or insignificant can be used to manipulate and use you. At best, just say no and thanks for the offer...avoid them. Worst still, when you do accept, ensure you tell your spouse every detail about it. When they are about to use it on you, walk away and cut that relationship, even if not permanently, but at least for some time. Give that relationship a breathing space so that you can reset and calibrate. Such temptation and manipulation normally come from friends, close relatives, your spouse trusted friends or acquaintances. Don't fall for the temptation of betraying your spouse, no matter what.

Always try to avoid elements that create distrust in your marriage. Do not betray the trust your spouse has in you and not for someone who you do not know that much. Chances are, that person who is making you betray your spouse will most likely disappoint you if you end up with them. There are findings that show spouses who left their marriage for another, ends up breaking up again within five years. So, why risk your precious marriage for an affair that may end in another short period?

We have spent time dwelling on trust because of its importance in a marriage. Trust is key to marriage and couples should try their best to build their home base on truths and not lies.

Anna Holloway – "Without communication, there is no relationship. Without respect, there is no love. Without trust, there's no reason to continue."

• **Short messages communication.** You can use this tool

to strengthen and build intimacy in your home. Write messages on sheets of paper, send electronic messages like a text, WhatsApp or Facebook to your spouse at intervals within the day or night especially when you both are not together. Tell them how you are feeling or some little chat on what's going on. Within the house, write messages on pieces of paper or sticky notes. It could be short romantic messages, like "I can't wait to kiss you," "Can you please come to the bedroom honey?" or after that heated argument, a small note on the chair that says, "Babe, I am sorry," or "Please forgive me, dear." Such messages can make your spouse smile, give them some relief or make them feel some good sensations.

- **Sexual communication.** This is another important aspect of communication in a home that improves intimacy. Couples need to talk about their sex life and sometimes discuss general topics relating to sex. In order to keep improving your sex life or when the sexual aspect of your relationship is not going great for instance, then both of you need to talk about it with an open mind and with a view of finding solutions. Don't just wish away your sexual problem, make some efforts at resolving it. Even when your sexual life is going great, there is always space for continuous improvement. Ask your spouse questions on how they feel during the process (sexual intercourse), what part do they enjoy most and if there are areas they would like you change or improve on. But like we mentioned earlier, be prepared to take the candid response on your part. Some of the responses from those questions could hurt you. Take those genuine responses as feedback that you may need to work on and improve for a better relationship.

- **Code Communications.** When a couple can develop some communication code just between the two of them, it strengthens their communication. Even if you both speak the same mother tongue, there are times when both of you will be among family members for instance and you want to say things to each other that no one else understands. Instead of calling your spouse aside, you can just use your code. It could be eye signals, body movements, words or even numbers and symbols. A pattern that can only be understood by just the two of you.

• **Communication in the presence of your children**. Children are very sensitive and could be attentive. Be mindful of the things you say generally in their presence. Kids try to imitate what their parents do. Do not yell at each other, not even in the presence of your kids. Don't use abusive words or phrases in their presence, whether jokingly, intentionally or unintentionally. Kids grasp these things fast.

• **Communication in the presence of family members and**

others. Managing how you talk to each other in the presence of other people is important. There must be mutual respect in the manner you talk. We have said this before: the use of foul language or abusive/derogatory words should not be tolerated under any guise. Whether it is a family member that lives with you in the house, or during a visit or an outing with other people (maybe friends, colleagues or associates), couples should always be mindful of the kind of words they use. Your wife/husband's interest, reputation and image should always take higher priority. Do not place others above your spouse. The way you portray each other, that is how those around you will see your spouse.

Try as much as you can to not to be involved in an ineffective way of communication that can or keep hurting your spouse. Before a marriage breaks, there is usually a breakdown of communication between both spouses. Communication is the bedrock of marriage. As we pointed out earlier, two separate grown adults, bred with different values, cultures, norms and beliefs came together as one to live forever. There is always bound to be conflicts. What is important is how these conflicts are managed and resolved.

Ensure you always maintain good and healthy communication habits. If there is no (good) communication between spouses, their interactions will be limited, and there will be no strong understanding between them. There will be no trust, no strong bond nor intimacy. There will virtually be no real relationship (what will exist between them will be a business relationship) and overall, no good marriage in a true sense.

If your marriage is going well, you will enjoy it. There is no reasonable amount of effort that is too much to put into a marriage.

Having an effective communication pattern is important in a marriage. Aside from the fact that it helps couples to avoid and solve minor marital challenges that may escalate in the future and possibly leads to break-up, it also helps couples to build a healthy, strong and intimate marital relationship.

William Paisley – "Communication is the fuel that keeps the fire of your relationship burning, without it, your relationship goes cold."

[CHAPTER FIVE]
SEX AND INTIMACY IN A MARRIAGE

Sue Johanson – "Sex is... perfectly natural. It's something that's pleasurable. It's enjoyable and it enhances a relationship. So why don't we learn as much as we can about it and become comfortable with ourselves as sexual human beings because we are all sexual?"

As communication is the bedrock of any marriage, so is sex the engine of a marriage... if not to all, but to a majority of adults. When you take away an engine from a vehicle, that vehicle becomes immobile on its own – cannot go forward, backward or sideways. It remains static. Over time, if left in that state, the parts get rusty and it will begin to decompose on its own. One can refer to the same scenario to marriage without sex. When you take away sex from a marriage, the marriage gradually dies a natural death until both spouses go their separate ways (unless they build other forms of intimacy and the no sex situation is based on mutual consent or an understanding).

According to **Sarah E. Clark**, a licensed therapist and relationship expert, "You can think of sex as a barometer of a marital relationship... when couples start to drift apart, lose their connection, take each other for granted, or build resentment towards each other, their sex life is drastically impacted."

Michele Weiner-Davis in her article titled The Sex-starved Marriage explained that "the sex-starved marriage is one in which one spouse is longing for more touch, more physical closeness, more sex, and the other spouse is thinking 'what's the big deal? It's just sex.' "

1 Corinthians 7:5 - "Do not deprive one another except with consent for a time, that you may give yourselves to fasting and prayer; and come together again so that Satan does not tempt you because of your lack of self-control."

When a spouse is sexually rejected, he or she most often shift rapidly to anger. In a marriage, each spouse could have varying sexual desires. The onus is now on the other member of the marriage to try their possible best in attending to those sexual desires. Couples should strive to always make continuous and significant efforts at satisfying the sexual urge of their partner instead of just shrugging them aside.

One possible means of achieving a better sex life in a marriage is through strong intimacy. This can be achieved with deliberate and committed efforts by both spouses and with better sexual communication. Couples should talk about those sexual challenges with the aim of finding a workable and acceptable lasting solution for sex issues in their marriage. Understanding each other's sexual needs is key in a marriage. Live with an open mind with your spouse and try to understand him/her better. Develop sexual rhythm between the two of you and be adventurous in your romance and sex life. All these are good for couples, to keep the sexual drive and desires burning.

Let me emphasize at this point that, although sex is very important in a marriage, sex alone cannot sustain a marriage. The idea that you can tie or hook someone with sex, is a farce. Because in the long run, after all the great sex, what next? That is why no matter how fantastic the sex is when the person you are trying to hook with sex alone has had enough of you, they tend to summon the courage and walk away. There are couples who have had great sex in their marriage but still break the relationship. The key is building stronger intimacy and let sex be the necessary icing on the cake.

MARITAL INTIMACY

Abhijit Naskar, author of The Bengal Tigress: A Treatise on Gender Equality – "Beauty is an illusion, created by Mother Nature to drive the human species in the path of reproduction. In reality, beauty is irrelevant to human life, especially in a relationship. What you today perceive as beautiful and special, over time, becomes not so special. That's how the human brain works. It is not beauty that keeps a relationship alive, it is attachment. Without attachment, a naked body is merely a lifeless sex toy."

Intimacy is a form of closeness in which partners feel secure and loved and in which communication and trust abound.

[1 Corinthians 7:3] - "Let the husband render to his wife the affection due her, and likewise also the wife to her husband."

As husband and wife, try to develop in your marriage: emotional intimacy, intellectual intimacy, heart-to-heart conversations, working together at common goals and spiritual intimacy. When couples are able to build intimacy in their home, they tend to easily surmount or even prevent some major challenges in their immediate family. What should have become a big issue, turns into something trivial and it is easily taking care of. Couples should share joys, fears, frustrations, sorrows and moments of anger with each other. That is, expressing those emotional states with their spouse. When the husband/wife shares intimate thoughts and feelings with his or her siblings (extended family), a friend, co-worker or online connections, he or she is betraying his or her spouse. Because such spots in your life are reserved for your spouse and should not be shared with any other person.

Genesis [2:24-25] – "Therefore a man shall leave his father and mother and be joined to his wife, and they shall become one flesh. And they were both naked, the man and his wife, and were not ashamed."

True marital intimacy usually involves being honest with your spouse and allowing yourself to be vulnerable to your spouse. This does not mean that you are weak; it displays your strength.

Using the **Champman** *five Love Language* can help couples build intimacy in their home. These languages include:

1.   Spending time together

2.   Touching, physical, affection, sex, etc.

3.   Affirmation, usually heart-to-heart conversations that are acknowledging, validating and appreciating.

4.   Acts of Service: like cooking, cleaning, taking care of the kids

5.   Material gifts, both large and small.

Couples can set goals together and work together at achieving those goals. Setting up projects and working on them together as well.

Spiritual intimacy is the strongest strength of a home. Do not be distracted to the extent of neglecting the spiritual aspect of your marriage. Always pray for your home. Remember the saying: "A family that prays together, stays together." When this is done genuinely, it is hard for that family to break. Imagine having a heated argument in your house and the two of you were angry at each other. Some couples will malice each other. When it is time for your regular or daily prayer, most likely, you will be forced to talk to each other and resolve whatever the difference is. Couples should try to study scriptures and pray together always.

Generally, doing things together – eating, watching TV, chatting, sleeping and waking – strengthens the bond in the home, and these help couples to understand each other better and build stronger intimacy.

In summarizing this chapter, sex is very important in a marriage. It is one of the purposes of marriage. A man/woman should not deny their spouse of sex and should try in their own possible best to satisfy the sexual desire and urge of their spouse. Couples should have good and healthy communication about their sex life, by being open about their weakness and work to resolve them in the best possible way. At the same time, sex should not be the only uniting factor between couples. That is why it is important for couples to build intimacy which can also help them to have a great sex life. Intimacy helps couples to strengthen their marital bond.

Keep the sexual drive in your home burning. Be adventurous; have quickies anywhere private around your home, away from the kids. Set up weekend dates; just the two of you. Studies show that couples who have sex regularly, live longer. Take time out to rediscover yourselves. Go on vacation, just the two of you and re-ignite your passion.

Good sex life in a marriage builds a better connection between spouses. If this is added with strong intimacy, then a long-lasting marriage is most certainly what that couple will be having.

Sheila Wray Grégoire – "Intimacy is about sharing something with your spouse that you don't share with anybody else. It's letting him/her in. It's laughing together. And it's also feeling that deep hunger for each other!"

[CHAPTER SIX]

MARITAL PRESSURES THAT BREAKS HOMES

"I, ______, take you, ______, to be my wife/husband, to have and to hold from this day forward, for better, for worse, for richer, for poorer, in sickness and in health, to love and to cherish, till death do us part, according to God's holy law, and this is my solemn vow."

After all the lovey-dovey, sweet dating and romantic nights, you will also be faced with marital pressures. Remember when they say marriage is for better for worse? Yes, that's exactly what it is. Challenges are going to come; it is inevitable. How those challenges are handled depends on how prepared and ready you are for them and some of the measures you and your spouse have put in place to avoid them altogether.

In this chapter, we examine some of the pressure points in a marriage and try to look at how best to handle them.

- **Marriage Preparation Phase**: we have discussed this in an earlier chapter. Because we are looking at issues generally in this category, it is noteworthy for us to mention and look at it once more.

There are bound to be arguments at this phase. But you should not let the arguments, misunderstandings and individual differences end that beautiful journey you are about to begin with your spouse. The bride and her family members may want XYZ while the groom and his family members want ABC. The couple wants it this way, while some of their friends and family or a certain section of the family wants it another way. All these results in misunderstanding, arguments and quarrels between spouses, that if not properly managed, can throw an upset into the marriage. Sometimes the couple may even want to call the marriage a quit when things get heated between them. Have you heard or remember phrases like "Can we just forget about this marriage thing," "It seems this marriage is actually a wrong idea," "The way you are behaving, it looks like we may have to call off this marriage?” These are emotional statements in the heat of the moment.

The best way to manage the crisis at this stage is for the couples to try and figure out what is best or suitable for them in the long run. In a bid to make decisions as to what is better in the long run, intending couples should answer questions like: “The issue at stake, is it going to result in additional expenditure? If yes, is it important, necessary or mandatory on the scheme of things? On the scale of things, of what priority is this thing that is the bone of contention?” Do not put yourselves in a future financial dilemma, take actions that the consequence will not have much negative impact both financially and otherwise on your home in the future or action that will not increase the bad blood between you and your spouse. This should guide your decisions at this stage. Couples should do what is best for them. Also, try not to burn bridges; you may need them later in life. This is where great caution and dialogue comes into play. Spouses should try their best to ensure the relationship between their siblings and other family members are cautiously handled and better or favorable decisions are reached.

- **SYNCHRONIZING MARRIAGE, WORK and OTHER ASPECTS of LIFE**: two grown adults just started living together. Life is no longer "I;" it is now, "us" and "we." What do we eat? Not what do I eat? Who cooks the food or gets the meal ready? Who does the laundry? Who does the dishes? Who cleans the house?

I recall a marriage where the couples started a divorce procedure immediately after they came back from their honeymoon. Each was used to different types of food. When they got back, in the process of deciding what they will eat and who prepares it, a quarrel broke out.

Some couples start their married life with house help. But for some, it is just the husband and wife. This form of pressure becomes present in a home, where both spouses are working. Combining work life and family responsibilities could be a very daunting task. For instance, while you are single, coming from work late or days with busy schedules, you could grab some pizza, soft drink or anything for yourself. Or when you get home, some leftover from previous days might just do the trick for you. But when you are married, it is no longer you alone and you cannot be living life in isolation. What will your wife or husband eat? Is it what the both of you desire? Then comes the second question after the decision of what to eat is made: who prepares the meal or get the meal ready? Is it a strict duty or responsibility of one spouse or anyone can cook the meal depending on who gets home first after work? When Mary and I got married, whenever I told her that I am closing on time at the office and getting home early, she would be happy. But that happiness turned to a complaint when she finally got home. Why, because, back then, once I got home from work, the only thing I really want to do is sleep. Then she comes and says, "How? You got home and the only thing you could do is to sleep without a thought of what to eat? I would simply say, "Sorry dear, I was tired. So, what do we eat?"

A couple once had a serious misunderstanding to the point that their parents had to step in to help resolve it. What led to their long quarrel? The man was always complaining that since they got married, he rarely eats freshly prepared meals; that the meals were always frozen. The woman worked with a corporate organization and always had heavy workload, so she uses the weekend to prepare their weekly meals and refrigerate them. The man, on the other hand, was among those who preferred freshly prepared meals. That led to series of quarrels that almost led to a separation.

Combining work and these house issues can be stressful for newlyweds and can put a lot of pressure on couples in general (those who have been together longer are able to work their way through this). Husbands and wives need to have an arrangement that can solve these challenges if they are facing one or two of these matters – agreeing on a workable plan and on what best suits each spouse. If both spouses are always having a handful at work, then it might be time to call in help that will help in taking care of these house chores and other matters in the house. Care must be taken when getting this help. Stories abound on how these third hands have broken or created havoc in a lot of homes; be it a relative or some neutral persons.

When getting help, some factors that should be considered include:

➢   Whether the person is going to live in the house with the couple or not

➢   The age of the adult and the gender to attend to some specific chores.

➢   If the person will not live in the house, the time of the day, and days of the week they can come to the house (weekend is mostly preferable were both spouses are in the house).

➢ The number of persons and who does what.

Choose an option that will work fine for both spouses, so long as their fears are allayed. The intention is to solve what may be a challenge in that home. Find a better solution rather than allow small issues to escalate and become a big problem that may lead to divorce.

Let us take Nigeria (Africa) for instance, where old traditions and cultures place the responsibilities of cooking and taking care of the home on the woman. When a woman does not know how to cook, for instance, she is generally considered not properly trained or raised or lacks a good upbringing. With the new age system and the ever demanding and challenging work environments, combining work, house chores and childbearing/child-raising, becomes a herculean task for women.

First and foremost, your wife is not by default your cook, or your housemaid or your child caregiver. She is your life partner (a helpmeet). As your wife, she has the same rights and privileges as you the husband. She should be respected and treated accordingly. Who prepares the meal is really not that important in my opinion. What is important is, whether the meal is tasty and ready when needed. The cliché of "I like fresh meals" should not hinder you from having a great home. For these categories of people who do not like meals that are refrigerated, freshly prepared meals are nice, delicious and

                    Vincent A. Omoamilor

could be healthier, but considering the time, cost and energy required on a regular basis, are fresh meals worth that value? This is a question you need to answer. A working mother, for instance, will not find it easy getting home after a tedious workday and then getting into the kitchen to start cooking.

In an instance where the couple do not have help with domestic activities, they can come up with an arrangement such that one of the spouse is responsible for the house meal preparation and dishes and taking care of the entire house, while the other spouse is responsible for taking care of the kids (if they have kids) and doing the laundry. Some couples even create a timetable such that these roles are alternated. Using options that enable couples to resolve these kinds of issues amicably are always preferable rather than building pressures on their spouse and letting negative vibes in the house leads to something else. Such negative feelings are displayed in the form of anger and continuous quarreling.

Couples should take a holistic view of their current circumstance by putting both partner's interests into consideration. They should come up with a convenient and workable plan that best fit the interest of both partners. It is a lifelong relationship; one party should not be made disadvantaged, living in grudges and left unhappy.

• **FINANCIAL CHALLENGES**: after sex, one major factor that breaks marriages is financial issues. Financial needs will arise in a home. Proper planning is very important. Most couple's financial challenges arise from:

1. <u>Already created financial disaster while getting married</u>. It is better not to go into debt to finance your wedding. If you are yet to get married, try as much as you can to avoid excessive debt as a result of a one-day event. The wedding ceremony is not an investment; it is a celebration. It is wiser to take from what you already have, to celebrate and be merry, rather than taking on huge debt.

2. <u>The values and morals of each spouse</u>. This tells how they see money or

what value they place on money. A spouse may be a saver, while the other is a spender. The man/woman might want more money and may want to live a life of affluence, while the other person is contended and is just fine with what they have.

As a couple, being able to put your heads together and plan your finance at the early stage of your relationship can save you a lot of headaches later. Avoiding debts and concentrating your expenditures on income-generating sources will help your family finance later.

Before Mike proposed to Yemisi, they were both living on credit cards and debts. Until one day, a friend invited them to a Personal Finance Seminar. When they got

                                    Vincent A. Omoamilor

back from this event, moved by the lessons they learned, they began to take notes of their expenditures. Mike found out that he spent an average of $40 on cigarettes in a week while Yemisi spent an average of $30 on cookies and chocolates in a week amid other frivolous expenditures. They both love to wear the trending fashions and use the latest mobile gadgets (all financed with their credit cards or other forms of credits. After the exercise, they both resolved to cut their expenses and start saving/investing. They got a financial planner who advised them on various investment options. So, they decided to start investing at least 100 dollars per month. Initially, it was tough for the two of them, as they had to give up some of their negative financial habits in order to cut their cost. But after a while, they grew from $100 monthly to $200 and soon, they were both making a combined investment of an average of $500 monthly. In about two years, the duo was having an investment worth $30k after paying off their debts and financing their wedding. This couple started their family with an investment worth close to $30k.

Compared to Frank and Maureen, the duo who was madly in love. They had no savings or investment. Frank used his credit card to order this beautiful diamond ring he used in proposing to Maureen. They took loans to finance their wedding. In the first two to three years of their marriage, they were spending an average of 40% of their earnings to service their

                    Vincent A. Omoamilor

debts. Soon, they began to feel the financial pressure and were always quarreling and yelling at each other.

Little habits of yours may be draining your finances. If you can take some time to evaluate your finance – create a budget, set savings and investment targets, cancel unused subscriptions, memberships and cards, stop or reduce credit card usage, negotiate your bills, etc. – anything to reduce cost and increase your income (you can even start a side business or part-time work...try to create strings of income).

If you compare those two families, the first family is in a better financial standing at the beginning of their marriage. They may face other marital issues at that early stage, but certainly not finance. While the second family started with a lot of financial burdens. These burdens, if not well managed, can spiral into other forms of marital issues.

A spender may look like a waster of resources and this may always bring misunderstanding and quarrel between both spouses. Having a joint account as a couple will enable spouses to track each other's expenses. There is the question of individual freedom and some level of privacy. But freedom may lead to a rivalry between spouses. For instance, both are working with different levels of income. When expenditures are separated, the spouse with a lower income may have some grudges or there may be some form of rivalry between them. This rivalry can lead to aggressiveness and quarrels, which will lead couples to have feelings of resentment towards each other. This kills the level of intimacy in that house and ultimately, no love. You do not need to rival your spouse in finance or any other thing. What belongs to your spouse, belongs to you. Even if it is on his or her name, both of you can enjoy the benefit of those belongings. So, you do not need to compete with yourself. A more complicated financial situation is when only one of them is earning. Envy, arrogance and rudeness will become a member of that home. Couples should try and manage such situations properly. It is common to find stories of divorce cases that originated from one of them losing his/her job, especially the male.

Spending secretly is another area that creates a crisis in marriages. This is either because the spouse is spending on things that he or she does not want their spouse to be aware of or they are spending excessively or lying about their financial standing. This creates trust issues in the home and couples begin to suspect each other. Think of it this way, an expenditure that you have to hide from your spouse is because it does not mean well for you and your home, which is most likely not ideal spending that will benefit your immediate family. That mainly explains why you have to hide it from your spouse.

Secondly, why do you have to hide your financial standing from your spouse? Do you have a problem when he or she knows your true financial position? Then try to solve that issue and clear off the financial secrecy from your home. Stopping financial secrets or stopping secrets generally in your home is a good habit you should cultivate and practice.

Extended family members can bring a financial burden to your home. You and your spouse should agree on how you spend on extended family members, whether such expenditure is approved by both spouses, and to what extent should your home bear the burden of extended family members.

The best time to make financial plans in a home is in the early days, months and years of marriage. As money is one of the leading causes of divorce, learn how to talk about money calmly. For couples that are planning to raise children, it is important for them to have investments/savings. Couples can set up investments that the return will fund their children's education or meet up their incremental financial expenditures overtime. Although it is not possible to know the exact amount such expenses may amount to, a budget with an estimate will do some magic. For instance, assuming it will cost you a total of $5,000 annually to take care of your child, an investment of $50,000 at an interest or return rate of 10% per annum will take care of that expenditure for your home without feeling any additional financial burden. That is, with this arrangement, you have successfully taken away the financial burden of raising that child. If you can make such an investment for every child, your home will not feel the financial impact of raising kids. If you can set up investments that the returns take care of the financial needs of your home, you can then use your salaries or regular income to focus on other projects. All things being equal, you can kiss financial challenges goodbye as far as running your home is concerned. Traditional investments to consider include fixed deposits, treasury bills, bonds, mutual funds, stocks, etc.

When you notice that the challenge in your home has to do with finance, examine the challenge and figure out the root or origin of the problem and take it from that point. Being able to identify the source is key to tackling such challenges. If the problem arose as a result of the personality of the couple (a saver versus a spender), it may be better for the partner who is a saver to be the one making the savings for the home. A proper budget or household budget should be made and followed by both partners to check the spending habit of the partner who is a spender.

When the challenge has to do with secrete expenditures, then it may be as a result of infidelity by one of the partners or in a more innocent circumstance, a partner is attending to extended family financial demands which the other spouse will either not agree to or tolerate. Such a partner needs to come out clean and start giving the other spouse an appropriate account of their expenditures.

Investopedia – 6 Marriage Killing Money Issues: "Studies have shown that people with more power are more likely to act selfishly, impulsively, and aggressively and approach others with less empathy." It suggests that "each partner in a marriage should ask themselves whether their behavior works towards the goal of a more kind, appropriate and equitable relationship or not?"

Minor financial challenges in a marriage, if not properly managed, degenerate to something bigger and sometimes result in divorce. Solutions to financial issues at home range from trying to manage your cost/expenses from the onset, to proper financial planning, savings and investment options to generate more income. **J. Ryan**, in her article, suggested the CPU (Cost Per Use) as part of the system to determine financial decisions in a home; for instance, a shirt that costs $10.00 that will be used 5 times has $2.00 per use. When you consider the value per use, you can then decide if you want to spend that value per usage. If such a guideline can guide a couple's financial decisions, that also will help them to minimize financial wastage.

As husband and wife, set financial goals together and work towards achieving them. Make time to discuss your money habits...spending, financial goals, savings and investment decisions and options, long term financial plans. You could even take a finance class together.

If your marriage is on the brink of collapse due to financial pressure and challenges, you may want to consult a financial counselor or coach (we will talk more on this in the next chapter).

If you are committed to a relationship, you and your partner owe each other a calm, honest conversation about each other's finances, habits, goals, and anxieties. It cannot be overemphasized that communication is the heart of every marriage. Good, honest, heart-to-heart communication can help couples manage a lot of challenges that include financial challenges and pressures, instead of letting them escalate and break your home.

- **SEX ISSUES**: this is also a leading cause of divorce. Sex issues in homes range from sexual unsatisfaction, incompatibility, to sex starvation, etc. that sometimes leads to extramarital affairs are currently dominant in a lot of home. We dedicated a chapter to this topic earlier because of its importance. Couples should always make cautious efforts at having a better sexual life in their home.

- **NO CHILD IN A MARRIAGE**: one of the major reasons for marriage and the mainstay of a family is the child. We could have said it is the major reason for marriage, but because people marry for different reasons – companionship, wealth and influence, etc. – this would not be the truth for all. The child is of great importance in a marriage and that is why some marriages break-up when they are unable to have a child after a certain period.

Below, we list some of the factors that bring externalities or third-party interference in a home.

FACTORS THAT BRINGS EXTERNALITIES INTO A HOME:

I.Financial issues

II.Quarreling and domestic violence,

III.Extramarital affairs and

IV.Inability to conceive

These four are the top marital issues that bring externalities into a home. Couples can hide or secretly manage the first three categories of family issues. Friends, family and acquaintances may not be aware. But how do you hide the fact that you have not been able to conceive or bear children since marriage? In certain cultures for instance, after two years or so, insinuations or questions will begin to come from family members, friends and acquaintances.

In Africa, for instance, extended family and siblings' pressures break a lot of homes when the couple is unable to have a child. Families faced with such challenges and pressures should try to wade off those pressures and find a solution to the problem and sustain their marriage in the face of those confrontations.

No matter how daunting these challenges are, remember these challenges are not peculiar to your home alone. About 10% of every couple is going through a similar challenge of conception. Most often, the pressure is placed on the woman when it comes to conception issues. But recent studies have shown that about 20% to 30% of infertile couples found out that the challenge is because of the male. While approximately 40% has both the male and female with fertility issues.

Male infertility hardly shows signs, except when the male semen is analyzed. So, it is very important for couples who are having conception issues to carry out a proper analysis of the male's sperm and check for issues like low sperm count or underlying medical problem(s).

Some of the factors that could be responsible for conception issues are:

A.   Couples not putting enough time and energy required for solving the problem. Work pressures like meeting deadlines, trying to generate more income, quarreling (misunderstanding between couples), etc., can deny couples of spending quality time with each other. Doctors recommend couples who are older than a certain age (35years – female, 40years - male) should try at least for 6 months before trying to seek medical help unless there are visible signs that one or both spouses may have fertility issues.

While those who are younger (35 years – female, 40 years – male), should try for at least one year. Sometimes all that is required of couples is to spend enough quality time with each other. About 80% of couples conceive after 6 months of trying, while approximately 90% conceive after one year of trying.

B.   Ovulation Irregularities. This could be endometriosis, which is characterized by painful and irregular menstrual flow, pain during sexual intercourse and infertility issues.

C.   Structural problems in the reproductive system on the part of the female and low sperm count, or medical problems on the parts of the male. Sperm must swim up from the cervix, through the uterus and into the fallopian tubes (where the sperm and egg finally meet). With a blocked fallopian tube, the uterine structural problem will prevent this process and therefore inhibit pregnancy from occurring.

Infertility in a woman can be caused by age, health problems (like PCOS), uterine fibroids, endometriosis, pelvic inflammatory disease and negative lifestyle factors.

While infertility in men may be caused by sperm gene defects, negative lifestyle choices (alcohol and drugs), toxins (lead, pesticides), STDs, diabetes, prostate or testicle problems. Various treatment for infertility includes drugs, surgery, intrauterine insemination (artificial insemination), assisted reproductive technology, and even third-party assistance, adoption and foster care can aid the couple in acquiring a child.

When conception is an issue in a marriage, couples should not let matters get to a breaking point. Discussions about the problem and searching/finding a possible solution to the challenge should be the right action and steps to take.

Your home is worth fighting for, and any reasonable steps that are within your capacity in order to keep your home is worth giving a shot. In the end, if you succeed in getting a positive outcome, you will be glad you did.

[CHAPTER SEVEN]

FIGHT FOR YOUR MARRIAGE

Darlene Schacht - "True love doesn't happen by accident. It's deliberate, it's intentional, it's purposeful and in the end, it's worth it."

We have touched on various aspects of the institution of marriage, ranging from the decision to get married to some of the factors and questions you should ask/answer when choosing a spouse and discuss some of the issues couples face in a home and try to proffer some solutions.

Before we conclude this book, let us emphasize the importance of working and fighting for your marriage. So long as the divorce has not been concluded, then it worth it to fight for your marriage and keep your family, even if you have gotten to a point where you have already given up on the marriage and you are already working on the exit route. It is not over as far as your marriage is concerned. Except in extreme and terrible cases, you do not have to use the exit route. Fight for your marriage.

If you are walking down the exit route and you still want to save your marriage and prevent it from crashing, just do these three things:

1.   Take those divorce papers or your exit routes and burn them.

2.   Make a commitment to keep your marriage.

3.   Start working on saving your marriage.

Your marriage should be a commitment without any contingency clause; like a covenant with unconditional promises. Storms in a marriage are inevitable, but quitting is optional. Take divorce off the table and be committed to your marriage 100% (till death do you part).

Ngina Otiende – "Marriage is meant to keep people together, not just when things are good, but particularly when they are not. That's why we take marriage vows, not wishes."

Learn to forgive your spouse unconditionally. That is the starting point of healing in your relationship issues. Forgiveness cannot be earned; it is given freely. You do not have to trust your spouse before you can forgive him or her, but in order to trust him or her, you must forgive. In as much as you need trust in your marriage to have better intimacy, you have to, first of all, forgive the wrongs of your spouse and begin to build trust over time.

Pride affects marriages negatively. In fact, pride has destroyed a lot of homes. But humility helps a marriage to grow stronger. In the book of **Esther**, King Ahasuerus dethroned Queen Vashti simply because of pride and Queen Esther excelled on the back of humility and submission. Be submissive to your spouse.

Your marriage should not be a marriage of only convenience; it should contain sacrifice (for better, for worse). You can disagree with your spouse in a healthy way. Instead of conflict, engage your spouse; fight together instead of fighting each other.

There are things that are in your control in the marriage and there are things that are out of your control. You have to deliberately work on your marriage and make it work. Commit to each other to make your marriage work for the long-haul. What is in your control in the marriage, do it. What is out of your control, just let it be and pray about it to change.

[**Philippians 4:6-7**] – "Be anxious for nothing, but in everything by prayer and supplication, with thanksgiving, let your requests be made known to God; and the peace of God, which surpasses all understanding, will guard your hearts and minds through Christ Jesus."

The daily simple purposeful things we do for or with our spouse can have a great impact and can either give marital fulfillment (the positive actions) or overtime, gradually separate the couple (the negative ones).

Dr. Kim Kimberling – "Very often, the lack of love is not because of a one-time sin but a subtle, ongoing pattern of behavior. Bitterness and love cannot live together in a marriage, each day, you and your spouse must decide which one gets to stay."

Setting the right boundaries and putting your home on a proper foundation can help your home and make a big impact.

❖ Set boundaries for your home – boundaries for in-laws, family members, friends and acquaintances. Set a separate identity for your family that should be recognized and respected. In-laws should give the couple space and the couple should set a boundary for their in-laws. The same applies to friends and acquaintances.

❖   Do not hurt your spouse – either physically by injury or fighting each other or by speaking badly/insulting your spouse. Don't allow people to speak negatively about your spouse in your presence – be it your friends or family members. It is extremely hard for our flesh and blood to forget the negative things we have told them about our spouse. Do not shout at your spouse or insult him/her no matter how angry you are.

[**Proverbs 15:1**] – "A soft answer turns away wrath, But a harsh word stirs up anger."

❖   Avoid keeping secrets from each other. Secrets build walls gradually in a marriage that destroys intimacy in the home. It also makes couples susceptible to temptation. Resist the temptations of keeping secrets from each other.

❖ Do not flirt with anyone other than your spouse. You may want to look up what constitutes flirting. It is important that you avoid doing them with anyone who is not your spouse.

❖ Do not let your family affect your marriage. Build and grow your own family and don't be distracted or misguided by their norms.

❖ Technological devices. Mobile phones and computers, with the presence of the internet, social media and mobile applications can steal the joy and intimacy in your home. Try to limit their usage and ensure they don't get to interfered excessively with your home. Do not replace your spouse with or give more attention to your technological devices.

❖   Your children.

[**Psalm 127:3**] - "Behold, children are a heritage from the Lord. The fruit of the womb is a reward."

The institution of marriage is for the children, wife and husband. Do not let the reward for your marriage becomes the obstacle of your marriage and ultimately, end it. The children will be affected when your marriage ends in a divorce; they are not better off in any way. They are important in the family, as well as you and your spouse. When your children grow, they will get married, go and start their own family and leave you and your spouse. A lot of couples neglect each other while they focus on their children. When these kids become adults and leave the house, the husband and wife will then appear to be so distant from each other as they have failed to build any form of intimacy over the years. This is one of the mistakes made by most parents: focusing their attention on the children and neglecting each other. Always remember that your (wife/husband) also have a life to live. So, your spouse is also very important and should not be taken for granted.

There is no perfect man or woman out there. This is a thought you should always hold at the back of your mind. With commitment from you both, you can build a great home together.

✓ Both spouses are to love each other. The man is placed with a primary responsibility to love his wife and love her independent of her behavior. Your spouse deserves your love and attention. She does not have to earn it. That is why it is unconditional love. When a man loves and honors his wife, his prayers are not hindered.

[**Genesis 29:18 and 20**] "Now Jacob loved Rachel; so, he said, 'I will serve you seven years for Rachel your younger daughter.' So, Jacob served seven years for Rachel, and they seemed only a few days to him because of the love he had for her."

✓   The woman should be submissive to her husband (even as both spouses need to be submissive to each other), your spouse deserves your loyalty and commitment. Similarly, neither does he have to earn them. Both major religions (Christian and Muslim) teaches this.

[**Ephesians 5:22 and 28**] "Wives, submit to your own husbands, as to the Lord. So, husbands ought to love their own wives as their own bodies; he who loves his wife loves himself."

[**Quran 4:34**] "Men are in charge of women by what Allah has given one over the other and what they spend from their wealth. So righteous women are devoutly obedient, guarding in absence what Allah would have them guard..."

✓   Couples need to drop unmet expectations of their spouse that get them angry, disappointed or frustrated and just love the person for who he or she is. Changing your ways, actions and expectations of your spouse; this can help you a great deal. Just see your spouse as he/she truly is and treat him/her that way.

✓   Create private time to spend and connect with your spouse. Find time to be together, even if you are not doing anything; you can both sit alone in the dark room silently and just connect. Search for what connects you as husband and wife and get involved in it often. You can also create fun times together, which include the children as well. All of these build the bond in the home.

✓   Serve your spouse. Focus your energies and thoughts on your spouse's wellbeing. Do not be selfish to him/her. This might be hard at first, but if you stay put at it, over time you will get used to it as you keep learning and practicing. If you take care of your spouse's needs, he or she will also take care of your needs without you asking. Marriages were spouses are selfless to each other rarely struggle, especially when they unconditional love and are committed to each other.

✓   Be transparent and even vulnerable to each other. Accept your spouse completely and be intimate with him or her. Not lying at all will save your marriage in the long run. Do not let lies create barriers in your marriage and prevent intimacy.

✓   Respect your wife/husband. Do not take your spouse for granted or always look down on him/her. Treat your spouse with dignity and respect, whether alone, amid friends, family members, or in public.

✓   Always talk with your spouse. It does not matter even if the two of you are quarreling. No matter how big the issue or argument is, maintain regular communication.

✓   Couples should carry each other's burdens. Partner with your spouse, love him/her, pray for each other, face every struggle and happy moments together.

IS IT TIME TO SEEK HELP?

Fighting for your marriage includes seeking help when the need arises; mostly when things have gone out of control after putting in your best.

If communication has broken down completely, no form of intimacy, there is abuse (both physical and emotional), extra-marital affairs, addiction and endangerment of the children (if kids are involved), I encourage you to hang in there and seek professional help. When these problems are escalating, it is advisable that both of you begin to attend teachings, seminars and conferences that relate to the main source of the issues you are having. It could be finance seminars or conferences if your major source of misunderstanding and quarrel is money, or a marriage/couple's retreats, seminars and conferences if you cannot be specific as to the source of the issues. If all of these are not able to kick start the conflict resolution process for you, then get a marriage and relationship expert service.

Be careful where you take marriage advice from. Do not take advice from someone who will sabotage your home directly (intentionally or indirectly/unintentionally). Try to get advice from someone who will be impartial. Seek the help of a professional counselor or therapist.

Most often, when families and friends get involved at this stage of the marriage (where there is a total breakdown of communication between spouses or some physical abuse or infidelity issues), they tend to end the marriage. Because, especially blood relatives, they don't forget negative things about your spouse. Getting the right acquaintance to intercede, who will be impartial, could be very difficult. That is why spouses should try their best to resolve their issues by themselves if they are not getting the service of a professional.

At first, both spouses or the member who wants to end whatever the challenge in the home, should make the move to kick-start the resolution process, by initiating conversation starters. From this point on, you can gradually build intimacy. If after all these efforts things continue to get worst and degenerates to a severe state, then you must get the service of a professional to help you.

 Vincent A. Omoamilor

[CHAPTER EIGHT]
PRAYER

Mother Teresa - "Let us love one another as God loves each one of us. And where does this love begin? In our own home. How does it begin? By praying together."

Most often, when couples live together without major challenges, they tend to under-value, or under-estimate the value of the peace and happiness they are enjoying and ignore prayer as a spiritual tool for their home. Peradventure, challenges show up, they become overwhelmed with such challenges.

Couples need to work on their spiritual life. Prayer is important in a marriage; to strengthen couples spiritually.

Thomas S. Monson - "Family prayer is the greatest deterrent to sin, and hence the most beneficent provider of joy and happiness. The old saying is yet true: 'The family that prays together stays together.'"

The benefits of praying together are what makes the family stay together.

Gordon B. Hinckley – "There are four pillars to a happy marriage: respect one another as individuals; (give) soft answers; (practice)financial honesty; (conduct) family prayer."

Bradford Wilcox in Faith and Marriage: Better Together? noted that "prayer helps couples deal with stress, enables them to focus on shared beliefs and hopes for the future, and allows them to deal constructively with challenges and problems in their relationship and in their lives. When I was a child, my dad had this small altar in the house where we all gathered every night to pray before going to bed. Before the prayers starts, he will ensure we were all present, and whoever was not, there needed to be a valid explanation. Growing up, I had personal experiences of God's power and miracles. This was partly made possible by a dad who created a norm of daily family prayer routine.

The benefits that accrue to a home when they pray together are enormous.

Research at Brigham Young University finds that "praying together as a family has many positive benefits, including reducing relational tensions and increasing feelings of closeness and unity."

Even if you do not know how to pray, a simple recitation of The Lord's Prayer and a chapter in the book of Psalms is a good starting point. As a Muslim, you can start by reciting 'surah al-Fatiha' and a short passage of the Quran. Whatever your religion, try to inculcate the habit of praying daily in your home.

Lesli White – 6 Benefits of Praying Together as a Family listed the following as some of the benefits of praying together as a family:

1.   Releases Deepest Hurts

2.   Heals

3.   Strengthens Communications

4.   Protects

5.   Strengthens Family Ties

6.   Builds Unity and Intimacy

In this article, the writer noted that we are in an era that is experiencing an unprecedented cultural attack on biblical values and the structure of the home, that prayer enables spiritual, emotional and physical healing in a home.

Pray for yourself, your spouse and your family. Always asking for God's protection and guidance over you, your spouse and your home in general. Pray relentlessly and don't ever get tired of praying. Pause for moments and say short prayers at intervals during the day, at work, business or even at school. Hold hands with your spouse in unison and pray with one accord. Pray about your goals, projects, agenda, work and family matters. Pray about everything, including the wellbeing of the family.

Do not wait until your family is into some problems before you start praying, always pray for your home, placing your family under the care of God.

Billy Graham – "True prayer is a way of life, not just for use in cases of emergency. Make it a habit, and when the need arises, you will be in practice."

Try to bond spiritually with your spouse. You may be surprised at the advantages it will give you. You can make it a daily early morning or evening routine. Neglecting the spiritual aspect of your family is not good. Regular study of scriptures and constant praying by both couples together can go a long way in uniting the home and strengthening the couple's intimacy.

Your home is worth fighting for. Couples should make deliberate efforts at saving their home. When you succeed in having a happy home, you will be surprised at the advantages it will give you.

Pope Francis - "May each family rediscover family prayer, which helps to bring about mutual understanding and forgiveness."

AMEN.

IN SUMMARY

This book examines the institution of marriage starting with an explanation of what marriage is about. It provides guidance on making the decision to get married, questions to ask your fiancée to enable you understand your prospective husband/wife. It further looks at delicate areas such as how to handle pressures from family members, in-laws and friends during marriage ceremonies preparations and event.

Communication in marriage is of vital importance and trust in a home is necessary for there to be success in the marriage and family unit.

Also, because of the importance sex and intimacy play in a successful marriage, this book would have been inconclusive without touching on that aspect.

Some marital issues usually lead to divorce and therefore they are dealt with extensively. The tricks to successfully navigate through a marriage on the verge of collapse and come out of the danger of divorce will prove useful to many.

Husbands and wives must be committed to their union, sacrifice for their home and always ready to fight for their marriage. They should seek help whenever the need arises.

The author encourages couples not to neglect the role of prayer in their marriages as it is important.

We sincerely hope you enjoyed reading this book and wish you a successful marriage.

Further Reading

- www.marriage.com

- www.focusonthefamily.com

- www.foryourmarriage.org

- www.marriagemissions.com

- Holy Bible